To

_____

From

_____

Date

_____

God and Me!

A Devotional for Girls Ages 4-7

Illustrated by
Olga & Aleksey Ivanov

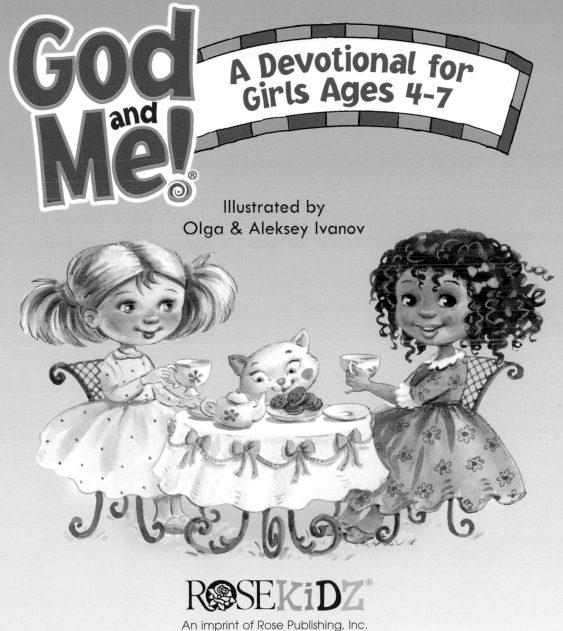

ROSEKiDZ®

An imprint of Rose Publishing, Inc.
Carson, CA
www.Rose-Publishing.com

God and Me!® A Devotional for Girls Ages 4–7
©2016 Rose Publishing, All rights reserved.

Contributors: Georgia Varozza and Jean Christen

RoseKidz®
An imprint of Rose Publishing, Inc.
17909 Adria Maru Lane
Carson, CA 90746
www.Rose-Publishing.com

Register your book at www.Rose-Publishing.com/register and receive
a free Bible Reference download.

Cover and interior design by Mary pat Pino
Illustrated by Olga and Aleksey Ivanov

Printed in South Korea   01   04.2016.APC

"To all children of God"

O.&A. I.

Day 1: God Helps Me to Know Him

Though you have not seen him, you love him; and even though you do not see him now, you believe in him... 1 Peter 1:8

Mommy was tucking Lexi into bed. Lexi asked, "Mommy, is God real? You and Daddy talk about God. But I can't see God. I can't hear Him. I can't play with Him. How do I know He's real?"

Mommy said, "That's a great question, sweetie. God is like the wind. We can't see the wind. But we know it's real! We hear the wind when it blows through the chimes on our porch. We see the wind making the tall grass in the meadow sway back and forth. We feel the wind on our faces. God is like that."

"We can hear and see signs of Him everywhere. Most of all, we can feel that He's real in our hearts when we ask Jesus to be our Savior. That makes us part of God's family."

Lexi thought about the leaves. "Oh, I know what you mean. The leaves move even though we don't see the wind. God is with us even though we can't see him!"

Talk About It!

What did Mommy say about God?

Have you ever been in a very windy day? What was it like?

How is God like the wind?

Try This!

What ways do you see wind or air acting in this picture? Count them!

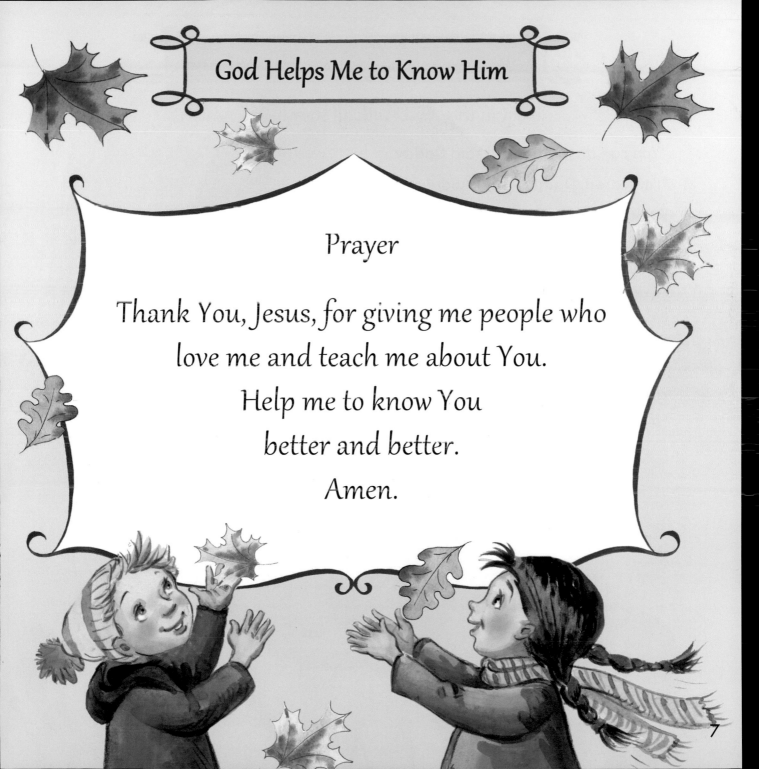

Prayer

Thank You, Jesus, for giving me people who love me and teach me about You. Help me to know You better and better. Amen.

Trust in the LORD with all your heart. Proverbs 3:5

"You can do it, Audrey," said Daddy.

"I'm scared, Daddy," said Audrey. "The horse is so BIG!"

Daddy hugged Audrey. He said, "I will lead the horse. I won't let him run. And I will stay right beside you. Trust me. Remember when you learned how to use your new wheelchair? It was scary, but you trusted me."

Audrey nodded. She remembered. She'd been scared then, too. But Daddy had helped her. He did just what he said he would do. And now, she could go just about anywhere in her chair!

Audrey gulped. She said, "Okay, Daddy, I trust you. Hang on tight."

Daddy held onto Audrey. He led the horse while Audrey sat high in the saddle. He stayed with her every minute.

When she was safely back in her chair, Audrey was so happy! "I trusted you, Daddy!" she laughed. "I knew you would be there. You helped me. Now I can ride a horse—with you!"

Daddy smiled. He said, "I am glad you trust me. But even better than trusting me is trusting Jesus. You can trust Him like you trusted me today. You can trust Jesus to always help you, be with you, and lead you."

Audrey hugged her daddy. She said, "I trust you, Daddy. And I will trust Jesus, too—always!"

Talk About It!

Why was Audrey afraid? How did Audrey's daddy help?

Who can we always trust to lead us and help us?

What are times when it's hard to remember we can trust Jesus?

What might help you to remember to trust Him all the time?

Try This!

Draw a picture of yourself having an adventure—riding a horse, climbing a tree, or whatever you like!

God Helps Me to Trust Him

Prayer

Jesus, please help me to remember
to trust You in every part of my life.
Thank You for leading me and
never leaving me.
Amen.

Day 3: God Helps Me to Be Thankful

*And do not forget to do good and to share with others,
for with such sacrifices God is pleased.* Hebrews 13:16 (NIV)

Give thanks to the Lord, for he is good. Psalm 107:1

Hailey's mom turned off the TV. The news was all about a big river that flooded. Hailey saw the pictures. She felt bad for the people in the flood.

"Mommy," said Hailey, "I feel sad for the children. They can't go back to live in their houses."

"It is sad," said Mommy. "Those people lost everything they had in the flood."

Hailey thought about all the food in their pantry. She thought about all of the clothes and toys in her room. "Mommy, could we do something to help them?" she asked.

"Absolutely, sweetheart!" said Mommy. "The Bible says that God is happy when we share what we have with others. Let's see what we can give!" she said.

Hailey hurried to her room. She filled boxes with books and toys. Then she and Mommy gathered blankets and food and clothes to share. Hailey felt good inside! And Mommy said that sharing made God happy, too!

Soon Mommy and Hailey had many boxes to load into their car. Hailey was thankful that they had so much to share! While Mommy drove, Hailey asked, "Mommy, can I write God a thank-you note? I want to thank Him for giving us so much to share. It makes me happy!"

Talk About It!

How do you feel when someone shares with you?

Read the Bible verses on page 12 aloud. A sacrifice is giving something away that we really like.

What is something you have given or shared? How did sharing make you feel?

Try This!

Make a thank-you note to God. Think about the things God gives you that make you glad.

Then write, "Thank You, GOD!" and draw pictures of those things. Hang your thank-you note picture in your room as a prayer of thanks to God!

God Helps Me to Be Thankful

Prayer

Dear God, thank You for taking care of me and my family! Please help us to care for others and share with them. Amen.

Day 4: God Helps Me toBe Obedient

Children, obey your parents in everything, for this pleases the Lord.

Colossians 3:20 (NIV)

Bailey loved to pretend that she was a famous space explorer. She liked to play in her room with her spaceships, imagining that she could fly her ship, Rocket, way beyond the stars.

She looked up at the sticker stars on her ceiling and thought. She said softly, "If I could jump on the bed high enough, Rocket COULD touch the stars. And if I'm really quiet, no one will know. Besides, my friend Hannah says that rules are made to be broken."

So Bailey jumped on her bed, higher and higher, when OOPS! she slipped and tumbled onto a pile of pillows on the floor, THUMP! Suddenly, Bailey was scared! The last time she disobeyed and fell off her bed, Papa had to rush her to the hospital to get stitches!

Bailey lay on her pile of pillows for a minute. She remembered what Mama had told her: "Our job to keep you safe. We love you very much. So we make rules to protect you, not to take away your fun." Bailey remembered how scared and worried her parents had been at the hospital. It made her sad.

Bailey closed her eyes. She prayed. "Dear God, I want to obey Mama and Papa. I don't want them to be scared. They love me. Thank You for keeping me safe this time! Please help me to obey Mama and Papa, even when I don't want to remember the rules. Amen."

Talk About It!

Why did Bailey's parents make a rule about jumping on the bed?

What rules do your parents make to keep you safe?

Is it true that rules are made to be broken? Why is it wise to obey?

Try This!

List some rules at your house. Then ask your parents to tell why they made those rules. And then, ask your parents to tell rules they had to obey when they were your age!

God Wants Me to Be Obedient

Prayer

Dear God, thank You that my parents have rules because they love me and want to keep me safe. Please help me to obey my parents—and be glad to do it! Amen.

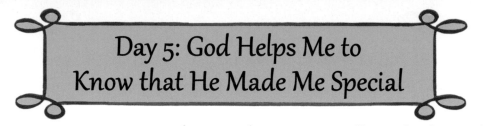

Day 5: God Helps Me to Know that He Made Me Special

In the same way, we are many, but in Christ we are all one body. Each one is a part of that body. And each part belongs to all the other parts. Romans 12: 4-5

Emma looked at the list of parts for the recital.

"AGAIN? I don't want to be a mouse AGAIN," Emma sighed. "I'm not special enough to be a Fairy Princess. I should quit. No one will notice if I'm not in the Christmas recital. No one pays attention to MICE!"

Emma smoothed her blue tutu and sighed again. She loved everything about ballet—except for being a mouse.

Samantha came and put her arm around Emma. "Why are you sad, Emma?" she asked. Samantha was older. She'd been the Fairy Princess for two years!

Emma sighed, "I wish I could be a Fairy Princess. I try my best every year! But I am a mouse AGAIN. I'm just not special enough to be anything else."

Samantha said, "When I was your age, I wanted the Fairy Princess part too. In fact, when I didn't get it, I cried. I told Mom I never wanted to dance again! But Mom told me, 'Small parts are just as important as the bigger ones.' She said the Bible teaches how we are each like a different part of a body. Some people are like the head or the hands or the feet. Without ALL of the parts, the body wouldn't work like it should. If just ONE little mouse is missing, our dance won't work right either! God made each of us to play a special part. We need to be the best we can be, right where we are!"

Emma looked up at Samantha. Slowly she said, "I guess it wouldn't work to have six Fairy Princesses and NO mice! Maybe I AM important. I will be the best mouse I can be!"

Talk About It!

Why was Emma feeling sad?

How did Samantha help Emma not be so sad?

Name some ways that God made you special. What gifts and talents did God give you?

Try This!

Play this game together. Take turns pointing to a body part. Ask, "What would I be like if I had no (feet)?" Each person gives an answer; try it with other body parts and answers. Then talk about ways each person in your family is special and important.

Prayer

Dear God, thank You for making
me special. You gave me a special part in this
world. Help me to remember to be the
best I can be.
Amen.

Do to others as you would have them do to you. Luke 6:31

Claire was so happy! Daddy was having tea with her and her stuffed animals. She loved dressing everyone up—even her Daddy—and talking about her day like a real grown-up.

"How was your day today, Claire-Bear?" asked Daddy.

"It was great, Daddy! There was a new girl at school today. She was eating lunch all by herself. I did not think that was right. So I invited her to sit with my friends and me."

24

"So did the new girl have lunch with you?"

"Yes, Daddy. I remembered how the Bible says to be kind, and to treat others the way we would want them to treat us. I wouldn't want to be all alone at a new school! And now, I have a new friend! Her name is Sasha. We are going to play together at recess and sit together at lunch tomorrow and maybe she can even come over for tea with my stuffed animals and me!"

Daddy touched Claire's cheek. "I'm proud of you, Claire-Bear. You did what the Bible says to do. You treated Sasha the way you want to be treated—and you made a new friend. Fantastic!" said Daddy.

Claire felt so happy! She gave her Daddy a big hug. She was glad to do what the Bible says to do. It always made her feel good and happy inside!

25

Talk About It!

When has someone been kind to you?

Tell about a time you were kind. How did it make you feel?

Think of something you really like for someone to do for you. How could you do that for another person? What is a way you can treat that person the way you like to be treated?

Try This!

Make Kindness Coupons! Cut sheets of paper into fourths. On one side, draw a picture. On the other, write a way you can be kind. Maybe you can take out the trash or help with the dishes. Give the coupon to someone you want to be kind to. Then be sure to do that kind thing!

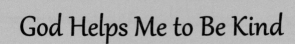

Prayer

Dear Jesus, please help me to
remember to treat people with kindness,
the way I want to be treated.
Thank You for being kind to me!
Amen.

Whatever you do, do it all for the glory of God. 1 Corinthians 10:31

Isabella had a problem. She told her mom, "There is a jump-a-thon at Sunday school next week! We're raising money so kids overseas can have Bibles. But even though I can jump rope, I always trip when other people are watching."

"I have an idea," Mommy said. "Practice jumping rope where there are a lot of people around. But don't look at them. Instead, look up. Think about God and talk to Him. Remember, He loves you, no matter how many times you trip."

"But what if I still trip after I practice?" Isabella asked.

"All God wants is for you to do your best," Mommy said.

Isabella practiced every day in front of people. She looked up and thought about God watching. She talked to Him.

On Sunday, she went to Sunday school and jumped rope with the other children. She tripped twice, but that was OK—she had done her best. And she knew that made God glad.

"Because we all worked together and did our best, we can buy Bibles for the children," said her teacher.

Isabella was very happy. She had done her best. She had helped someone. And she knew God was glad!

Talk About It!

What is something easy for you to do? What is something hard for you to do?

Who can we think about and talk to, no matter what we are doing?

Ask someone to tell you about a time when she did her best.

30

Try This!

Help Isabella find her jump rope. Use your finger to trace the path from Isabella to her rope. How many other people are jumping? Trace the paths to each of Isabella's friends, too.

God Helps Me to Be My Best

Prayer

Dear God, thank You that
I can always talk to You. Thank You for
always loving me. And thank You for
helping me to do my best.

Amen.